A Short, Illustrated History of...

INVENTIONS

Clive Gifford   Rita Petruccioli

ROSEN PUBLISHING

Published in 2025 by The Rosen Publishing Group, Inc.
2544 Clinton Street, Buffalo, NY 14224

First published in Great Britain in 2020 by The Watts Publishing Group

Series Editor: Amy Pimperton
Series Designer: Lisa Peacock
Illustrations by Rita Petruccioli

Cataloging-in-Publication Data

Names: Gifford, Clive, author. | Petruccioli, Rita, illustrator.
Title: Inventions / by Clive Gifford, illustrated by Rita Petruccioli.
Description: Buffalo, New York : Rosen Young Adult, 2025. | Series: A short, illustrated history of... | Includes glossary and index.
Identifiers: ISBN 9781499476422 (pbk.) | ISBN 9781499476439 (library bound) | ISBN 9781499476446 (ebook)
Subjects: LCSH: Inventions–History–Juvenile literature.
Classification: LCC T15.G56 2025 | DDC 609–dc23

Manufactured in the United States of America

CPSIA Compliance Information: Batch #CSRYA25.
For further information, contact Rosen Publishing, New York, New York, at 1-800-237-9932.

Contents

Creative Curiosity

Human beings are very curious creatures. They have always looked at the world around them and tried to find creative ways to use their surroundings to make life easier or safer. This curiosity helped ancient peoples learn how to farm the land and grow crops so they could live in one place. It also led to people making useful new materials, such as iron, bronze, and glass, and to build the first boats and ships, allowing travel across water to new lands.

The inventions that prehistoric people made laid the foundations for future ingenious inventions.

An early potter's wheel

People have proven remarkably skilled at taking one invention and improving it or using it for a quite different purpose. The first wheels were invented in ancient Mesopotamia (present-day Iraq) around 5,500 years ago. They weren't used for transportation, but as potters' wheels for spinning clay pots.

Within a few years, people had the inspiration of turning two wooden wheels on their side, fitting a rod between them — called an axle — and inventing the first wheeled transportation.

Early wheeled carts were often pulled by oxen.

Ingenious people have invented thousands of different objects and machines. Some are small and simple, but clever, such as the paper clip or can opener. Others are huge and complex, such as powerful supercomputers, giant jet airliners, or spacecraft like the International Space Station. A Boeing 747 airliner, for example, has over six million parts! Some inventions are thought up in a single moment, while others take years or even decades to develop.

This book is packed full of moments of ingenuity and hard work that led to important inventions that have helped to shape our world.

Ancient Tools

Hand tools, such as scrapers made of sharpened stone, have been used for tens of thousands of years. Early people were nomadic. When people began to settle in one place, new tools were invented to help with farming and constructing buildings.

The scratch plow was the first type of plow. Invented in the Middle East about 7,000–7,500 years ago, it used a sharpened piece of wood pulled behind oxen or other animals to dig a long furrow in the ground to plant seeds. The plow made it easier to farm larger areas of land and produce bigger crops to feed more people.

Bigger farm fields meant the need for more water. Farmers in ancient Egypt and Mesopotamia, as well as the Minoans on the Mediterranean island of Crete, invented the *shaduf* at least 4,000 years ago. It consisted of a wooden frame on which a long wooden pole acted as a lever. A bucket or bag made of animal hide on one end of the pole was lowered into a river or lake to raise water up to ground level. Shadufs are still used to this day in some places.

As settlements grew in size, building work increased in scale. Machines were needed to raise large stone blocks and other heavy materials. The ancient Greeks invented cranes around 550 BCE. These ran ropes around a series of wheels, called pulleys, to increase lifting force.

Ancient Romans, wanting to lift even bigger loads to build impressive structures, such as aqueducts, invented *polyspastos* cranes. These were powered by enslaved people walking inside a wooden treadwheel, a little like a human-sized hamster wheel. Some Roman cranes could lift 13,000 pounds (6,000 kg).

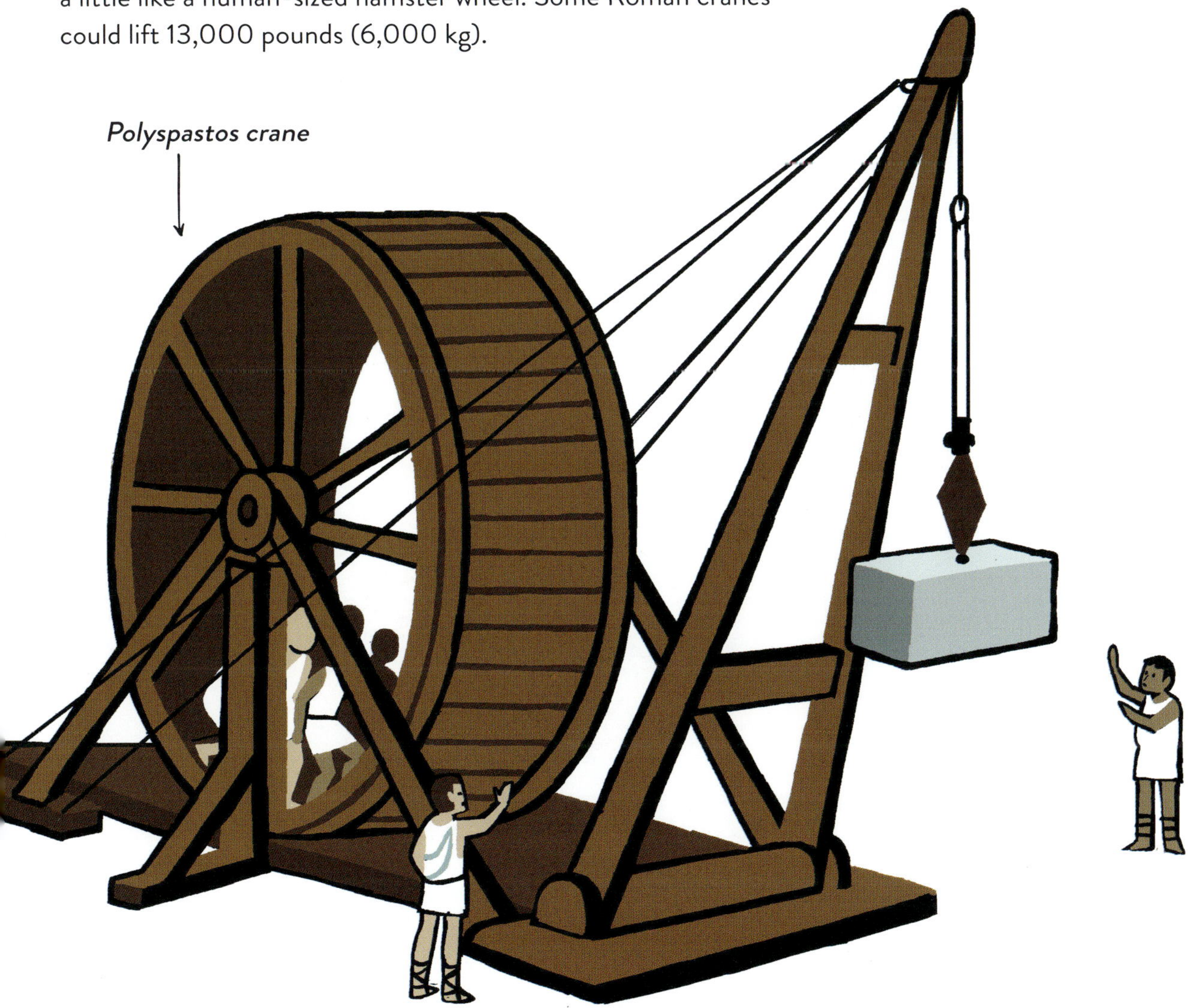

Ancient Chinese Inventions

Many objects we take for granted today were first invented in ancient China — from the toothbrush and compass to the wheelbarrow. Two of the most important ancient Chinese inventions were paper and gunpowder.

In CE 104, a Chinese court official named Cai Lun (c. CE 50–121) described how paper was made. Plant fibers, such as tree bark, were soaked with shredded rags and then mashed to a pulp. This was spread on to frames and dried to form thin, flexible sheets that were easy to write on.

← *Jiaozi*

The Chinese used their new invention to make the world's first paper banknotes, called Jiaozi, which were easier to carry than heavy bags of metal coins. They also created paper sheets 35 inches by 24 inches (90 cm by 60 cm) — the world's first toilet paper — which was used by wealthy people.

Around CE 850, the Chinese experimented with mixing charcoal and sulfur with a substance called saltpeter, which is found in certain types of rock and soil. The end result was the first gunpowder. It burned fiercely when lit. Short bamboo tubes attached to arrows were filled with gunpowder to make fire arrows.

Fire arrow

More explosive versions of gunpowder were developed by about CE 1000. When packed into a large bamboo tube and lit, the explosion was strong enough to fire an arrow or sharp pieces of metal at an enemy. Later inventions used gunpowder to fire shot from cannons and bullets from rifles and handguns.

Modern fireworks

Fireworks

By 1100, the Chinese were launching paper tubes of gunpowder into the air to produce startling explosions, light flashes, and smoke. Powdered iron added inside the tube produced spectacular sparks as it burned. Over time, different chemicals were added inside fireworks to produce colors: copper for blue, calcium for orange, and barium for green.

Printing Press

Block printing was first practiced by the ancient Chinese, who carved the characters forming a page into a solid block of wood. The block was covered with ink or paint and then pressed onto paper or silk. This allowed copies of the same page to be printed one after the other.

While woodblock printing was quicker than copying out long documents by hand, carving an entire page of characters out of wood took a long time and was costly. As a result, there were few books or other text documents produced.

In China around 1040, movable type printing was invented. This used individual characters made of clay that were arranged in wooden frames to form a page, which could then be printed. Each clay letter could be reused on a different page. Clay proved fragile, and within several centuries, printers in Korea were using movable type characters made of bronze.

← *Movable clay printing blocks*

Between 1440 and 1450 a German blacksmith and jewelery maker, Johannes Gutenberg (c. 1400–68), developed his own version of movable type printing. He built a wooden printing press similar to presses used to squeeze grapes and olives in farming and developed an oily ink that stuck well to paper. The ink used ingredients including oil from walnuts and soot. This was rolled over the metal type, which was then pressed down firmly on to paper.

Gutenberg's innovations spread through Europe. Suddenly, books, posters, and pamphlets could be printed easily and cheaply. As a result, news and information spread more quickly and widely than before, with the first newspapers printed in Europe in the 1600s.

Johannes Gutenberg's printing press

Scientific Advances

The printing press was crucial to the development of scientific knowledge around the world. Access to the scientific findings of others inspired and then accelerated the pace at which inventions and discoveries were made and shared.

Clocks

People have long had a passion for telling the time: using the position of the sun, falling sand in an hourglass, the flow of water in a clepsydra (water clock), or mechanical clocks powered by springs or falling weights. However, these systems weren't very accurate and were often off by many minutes each day. Most medieval mechanical clocks did not have minute or second hands.

Hourglasses filled with sand were popular devices for measuring fixed periods of time.

Around 1602, Italian scientist Galileo Galilei (1564–1642) studied pendulums – swinging weights hung from a fixed point. Galileo discovered that a pendulum weight always took the same amount of time to complete a swing whether its swing was long or short. In 1656, Dutch scientist Christiaan Huygens (1629–95) used this fact to build a clock that kept the time by using a swinging pendulum.

Hugyens's clock featured a gear called an escapement that helped make the clock's hands turn as the pendulum swung, creating a tick-tocking sound. The escapement also transferred energy to the pendulum to keep it moving.

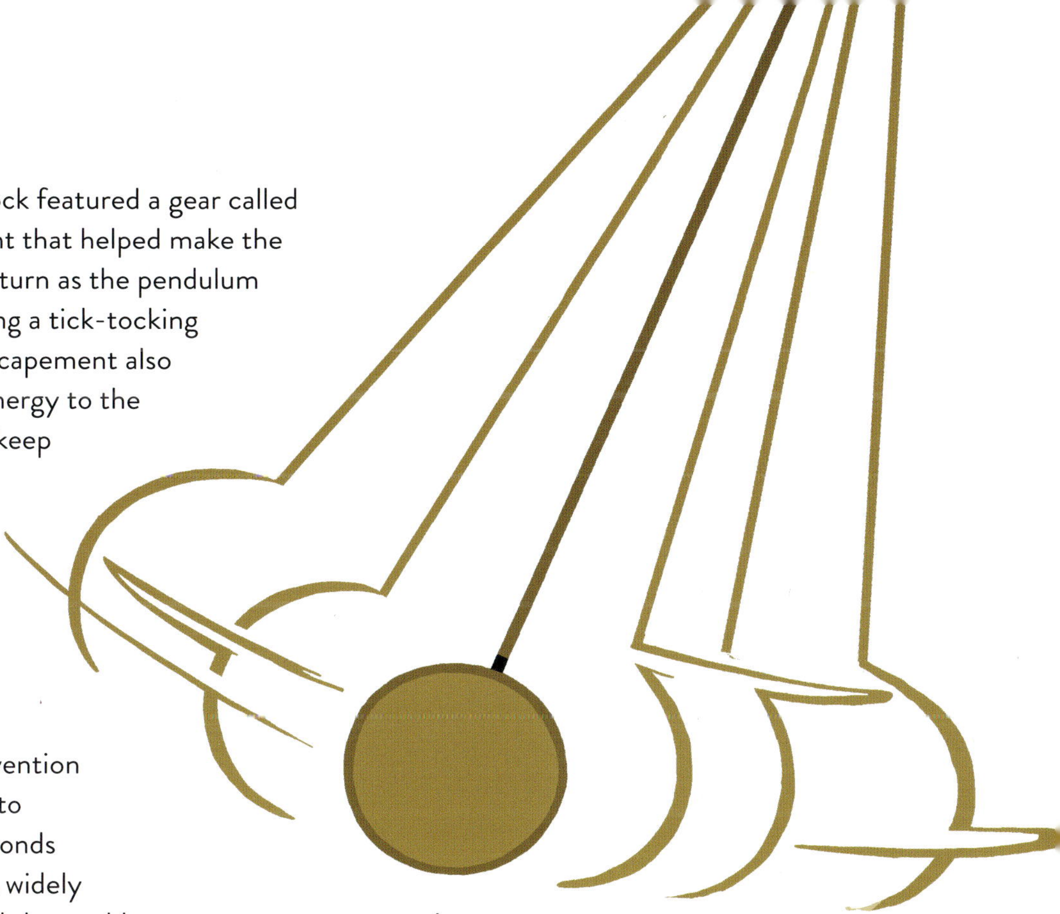

Pendulum

Huygens's invention was accurate to around 15 seconds a day and was widely copied around the world. Tall grandfather clocks, for example, contain a swinging pendulum inside their wooden cabinet.

Christiaan Huygens

Quartz Clocks

Pendulum clocks remained the most accurate timekeepers available until the invention of quartz clocks in 1927. These use a battery to pass electricity through a sliver of quartz crystal. The crystal vibrates a precise number of times per second, which can then be converted into an accurate time.

Steam Engines

Steam engines were first used as water pumps (mostly in mines, which could get waterlogged). In 1698, English engineer Thomas Savery (c. 1650–1715) created a steam pump that is thought of as the first steam engine to be put to work.

English blacksmith Thomas Newcomen (1664–1729) invented a pump engine design in 1712 that used steam to push a rod called a piston up and down inside a cylinder. In the 1760s, Scottish engineer James Watt (1736–1819) began making improvements to Newcomen's engines, which used a lot of coal as fuel but produced relatively little power. Watt's work had a huge impact, making steam engines much more powerful, useful, and reliable.

James Watt and his steam engine

Watt built engines with a separate cylinder, called a condenser, for steam to cool. This helped the engine waste a lot less energy and work faster. He also invented double-acting steam engines, where the pistons produced power when they moved both up and down. Previous engines only produced power in one piston direction. Many of Watt's engines used only a quarter of the coal of a Newcomen engine.

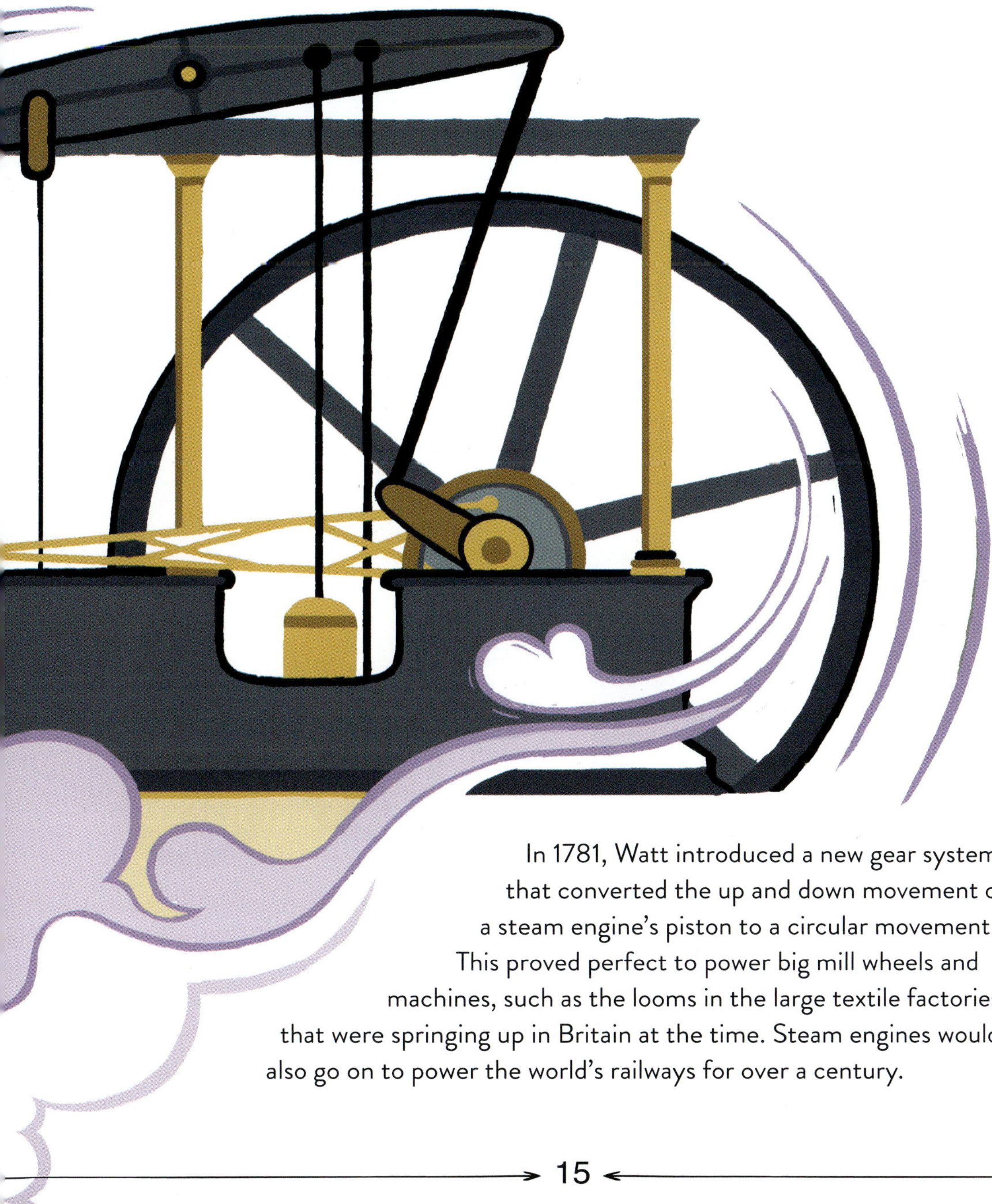

In 1781, Watt introduced a new gear system that converted the up and down movement of a steam engine's piston to a circular movement. This proved perfect to power big mill wheels and machines, such as the looms in the large textile factories that were springing up in Britain at the time. Steam engines would also go on to power the world's railways for over a century.

Locomotives

In England in 1829, a competition was held to find the best locomotive (self-propelled steam engine) to pull carriages full of passengers. The Rainhall Trials attracted a crowd of 15,000 spectators as different locomotives competed. Up until that time, locomotives had been mostly used to haul coal from mines.

The *Rocket*, designed and built by English engineer Robert Stephenson (1803–1859), outperformed all the other contenders including the *Perseverance* and the *Novelty*. It was more reliable than its rivals, which broke down frequently. It also reached 30 miles per hour (47 km/h) along the track — faster than any land vehicle before it. When the 31-mile-long (50 km) Liverpool and Manchester Railway opened the following year, the *Rocket* pulled passengers in carriages along it for four years.

Steam locomotives featured boilers supplied with water, which was heated by burning coal or wood in a furnace. The water turned to steam that expanded and pushed the pistons, which in turn drove the locomotive's wheels. Steam locomotives were common on railways well into the 20th century, until new trains powered either by electricity or diesel engines took over.

Bullet Trains

In 1964, the first high-speed electric train went into service between the Japanese cities of Tokyo, Nagoya, and Osaka. Running on its own smooth track, the sleek *Shinkansen*, or "Bullet Trains," raced along at speeds of 130 mph (210 km/h) and slashed journey times by more than half. Some of the locomotives proved so reliable that they kept on running until 1999.

Bicycles

Wheels had been around for over 4,500 years before German inventor Baron Karl von Drais (1785–1851) arranged two of them, one in front of the other, on a frame to provide personal transportation. His 1817 invention became known as a *Draisienne*. It had handlebars and a saddle, but no pedals. Riders moved by paddling their feet across the ground.

Draisienne

When pedals on bicycles arrived, they were fitted directly to the front wheel to create machines called velocipedes. These had no gears, so every complete turn of the pedals turned the wheel around once. To make faster bicycles, people built larger and larger front wheels. Penny farthings made by James Starley (1830–81) and others in the 1870s had giant 5-foot-tall (1.5-m) front wheels, making riding unstable and scary.

The penny farthing was named after two British coins: a penny and the much smaller farthing.

Starley's nephew, John Kemp Starley (1855–1901), created a safer bicycle design with two similar-sized wheels in 1885. He placed the pedals underneath the rider and linked them to the rear wheel via a metal chain made of lots of links. The diamond-shaped frame was stronger and lighter, and Starley's safety bicycle was far easier to ride. The design was adopted all over the world.

Safety bicycle

In the 20th century, lots of new designs of bicycles were invented. Frames got lighter, and new gear systems allowed riders to pick how fast or slow they wanted to pedal to travel at a certain speed. Light but sturdy BMX bikes were first built in the 1970s for off-road racing around dirt tracks.

Mountain Bikes

In the 1970s, a group of American cyclists who liked to ride over hills and rough ground started to build their own bikes with chunky tires and strong frames to withstand all the bumps. This resulted in the first mountain bike, the Specialized Stumpjumper, which went on sale in 1981.

Computers

Charles Babbage (1791–1871) was way ahead of his time when he designed (but only partly built) a mechanical computer in the 1830s and 1840s powered by a steam engine. In 1842, Babbage's friend and mathematician Ada, Countess of Lovelace (1815–52), wrote a series of instructions for Babbage's Analytical Engine (just like modern computers use programs), making her the world's first computer programmer.

Charles Babbage and Ada Lovelace

In the 1940s, engineers harnessed the power of electricity to create the first general purpose electronic computers. These giant machines could perform the complex math needed for weapons design, weather forecasting, and other tasks. ENIAC* in the United States was one of the first and most successful, running from 1946 to 1955. It was as long as a basketball court and weighed 30 tons (27 tonnes).

* ENIAC stands for Electronic Numerical Integrator and Comput

ENIAC could only run one program at a time, and changing programs meant that lots of its parts had to be rewired by staff known as "computers." Once programmed, though, it was fast for its time. Math that would take a skilled person 20 hours could be completed by ENIAC in under 30 seconds.

The invention of electronic parts, such as the transistor in 1948 and the microchip in 1959, helped computers shrink in size and cost, yet increase in power. The hard disk drive (1956) and the computer mouse (1963) helped make computers easier to use. Microprocessors were developed, which were complete computing systems on a single microchip. By 1997, all of ENIAC's abilities could be performed by a single microprocessor measuring 7.5 mm by 5 mm — smaller than a fingernail!

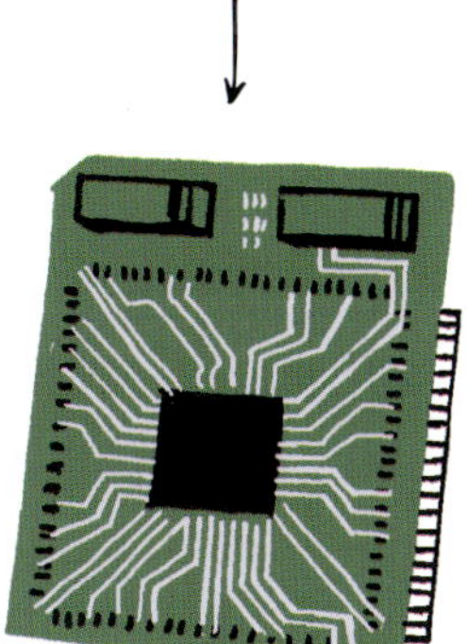

Plastic

Plastic is everywhere today, but it didn't exist 200 years ago. In 1856, Englishman Alexander Parkes (1813–90) invented Parkesine — a plastic material made from plant fibers. In 1870, John Hyatt (1837–1920), assisted by his brother Isaiah, produced a new version of Parkesine that they called celluloid. It was used to make lots of different products, from billiard balls to false teeth.

Billiard balls

The first plastic made from coal and oil was Bakelite in 1907, named after its inventor, Belgian chemist Leo Baekeland (1863–1944). It was the first plastic that could be heated and molded, but once it cooled it didn't change shape. Following Bakelite's success, further plastics were invented from coal and oil, including polystyrene in 1929 and polythene and polyvinylchloride (PVC) in 1933.

Bakelite telephone

Plastic proved lightweight, cheap to produce, easy to shape, and long-lasting. Some types were great at keeping rain off. Because plastic didn't conduct electricity, it was also used heavily in electrical goods and wiring. In 1935, American chemist Wallace H. Carothers (1836–1937) invented a new plastic fiber that became known as nylon. It was tough and hardwearing and was used to replace natural silk in clothing and parachutes. Nylon is now used for thousands of products, including clothing and cookware.

Silk was hard to come by during World War II (1939–45), so the military began to use nylon to make parachutes for their troops.

Plastic Planet

Plastic's durability wowed people at first. Now, it's a big problem. Many plastics can take 500–1,000 years to biodegrade. This means they stick around on land and in air and water, where they can harm and kill creatures and pollute our planet. More than 9 million tons (8 million tonnes) of plastic enter the ocean each year.

Motor Cars

Land vehicles were powered by steam or animals until Belgian engineer Étienne Lenoir (1822–1900) invented an engine in 1860 that burned fuel and air inside a metal cylinder. Various people improved upon Lenoir's design to build internal combustion engines far smaller than a steam engine, yet capable of producing more power.

In 1885, a German engineer, Carl Benz (1844–1929), fitted an engine to a three-wheeled vehicle he designed to create the first practical motor car. Benz's Motorwagen had a top speed of 10 mph (16 km/h), but no steering wheel. Instead, it was steered with a lever like a boat tiller.

Bertha Benz in the Motorwagen with her sons Richard and Eugen

In 1888, Benz's wife, Bertha (1849–1944), took a Motorwagen for a spin with her two young sons and became the first long-distance driver. She drove 110 miles (180 km) through Germany, using a hatpin to clear blocked fuel tubes and stopping off at a pharmacy for fuel as there were no gas stations!

Bertha Benz's epic trip gained much publicity, and Benz's next car, the four-wheeled Velo, was a big success with 1,200 built. Other carmakers sprang up in Europe and the U.S., including Henry Ford (1863–1947). He developed moving assembly lines to speed up car-making. His Model T Ford became the first car to sell a million units. Between 1908 and 1927 over 16.5 million were built. Today, more than 1.1 billion motor vehicles can be found on the world's roads.

Windshield Wipers

In 1903, American Mary Anderson (1866–1953) invented a car windshield wiper. To operate it, the driver used a lever inside the car to pull a rubber blade across the windshield. The first electric wipers were invented 14 years later by American Charlotte Bridgwood (1861–1929).

Electric Light

When electricity flows through certain materials, it generates lots of heat that can cause the material to glow and give off light. Many scientists experimented with making incandescent lights in this way. One of the first to be successful was English scientist Joseph Swan (1828–1914). In 1860 he passed electricity through a thin carbon thread, called a filament, to produce light.

Swan found that the filament often caught fire as it heated up. Because fire needs oxygen from air, Swan sealed the filament in a glass container from which almost all of the air had been removed. His improved light bulbs lit the first home (his own in Gateshead, England, in 1879) and first public building (London's Savoy Theatre, in 1881).

Around the same time, American inventor Thomas Edison (1847–1941) was desperately working on producing his own practical light bulbs. After more than 4,000 experiments with different materials, Edison found that bamboo filaments could glow for more than 1,200 hours. At the time, carbon filaments lasted only 40 hours. Edison and Swan battled as rivals for a short time before they joined forces to produce Ediswan bulbs, which sold in the thousands.

Thomas Edison holding an Ediswan light bulb

Incandescent light bulbs lit up the 20th century, but they wasted a lot of energy as heat. New energy-efficient lamps were developed. One type, the Compact Fluorescent Lamp (CFL), was invented in 1976 by American engineer Edward Hammer (1931–2012). This spiral-shaped lamp is filled with gas. When electricity is passed through it, a coating inside the bulb emits a glow. CFLs use around 70 percent less energy than incandescent bulbs.

Neon

Frenchman Georges Claude (1870–1960) discovered that electricity passed through neon gas gave off a bright, orange-red light. He invented colorful neon lights in 1910, which were used in advertising signs and displays.

Telephone

In the 1860s and 1870s, inventors such as Elisha Gray (1835–1901), Antonio Meucci (1808–99), and Johann Reis (1834–74) all raced to devise practical ways of sending speech and sounds as electrical signals long distances along wires. Alexander Graham Bell (1847–1922) won the race, patenting his telephone system in 1876.

Bell's system used a metal cone to collect sound waves as vibrations. The vibrations were turned into pulses of electricity that could travel along electrical wires to a receiver. There, the pulses were converted back into sounds that were played through a small loudspeaker.

First Words

The first words spoken by telephone used Reis's primitive *telephon* in 1861. The German sentence translated to "The horse doesn't eat cucumber salad!" Bell's first words over his system were, "Mr. Watson, come here — I want to see you." In 1915 Bell repeated his words, but this time with him in New York and Mr. Watson (1854–1934), his former assistant, in San Francisco. It was the first call made across the entire United States.

Alexander Graham Bell

Within five years of Bell's invention, there were almost 50,000 telephones in the U.S. At first, each telephone was connected directly to another by a fixed line. The invention of switchboards in the late 1870s allowed operators to enable calls between different lines by plugging one telephone line into another. Emma Nutt (1860–1915) became the world's first female switchboard operator in Boston in 1878.

From the 1890s to the 1970s, most switchboard operators were women.

The use of telephones boomed, including the arrival of coin-operated payphones. The first was installed in 1889, in the town of Hartford, Connecticut, by inventor William Gray (1850–1903). Long-distance phone calls became possible, while the first transatlantic phone call was made in 1927 between New York and London.

Almost all telephone calls were made along fixed land lines until the invention of the cellular mobile phone, which used radio waves to connect calls. The first mobile phone, the Motorola DynaTAC 8000X, went on sale in 1983, ten years after a prototype was first demonstrated. It cost over $3,000, weighed 28 ounces (790 g) and stood 13 inches (33 cm) tall. Mobile phones developed rapidly: slimming down, gaining touchscreens, and in the 2000s, becoming smartphones running programs called apps.

Sound Recording

Sound travels as a series of vibrations through the air. In 1877, Thomas Edison produced a prototype device that could capture sound and play it back. The very first recording was Edison speaking the nursery rhyme "Mary Had a Little Lamb."

The sounds of his words vibrated a metal needle that dug into a layer of tinfoil wrapped around a cylinder. When the cylinder was replayed, dents in the tinfoil made a different needle vibrate, recreating the original sounds. Edison named his invention the phonograph.

Thomas Edison and his phonograph

Always seeking to improve his inventions, Edison replaced the tinfoil — which could only be replayed a handful of times — with cylinders coated in a thick layer of wax. Each wax cylinder had to be recorded individually and could only hold around two minutes of sound.

In the late 1880s, German American inventor Emile Berliner (1851–1929) invented flat gramophone discs as an alternative to phonograph cylinders. Berliner's discs could be mass-produced in a factory and became very popular. Gramophone discs developed into records made of vinyl plastic. Long playing (LP) records could hold 50–55 minutes of music on their two sides.

Emile Berliner's gramophone disc

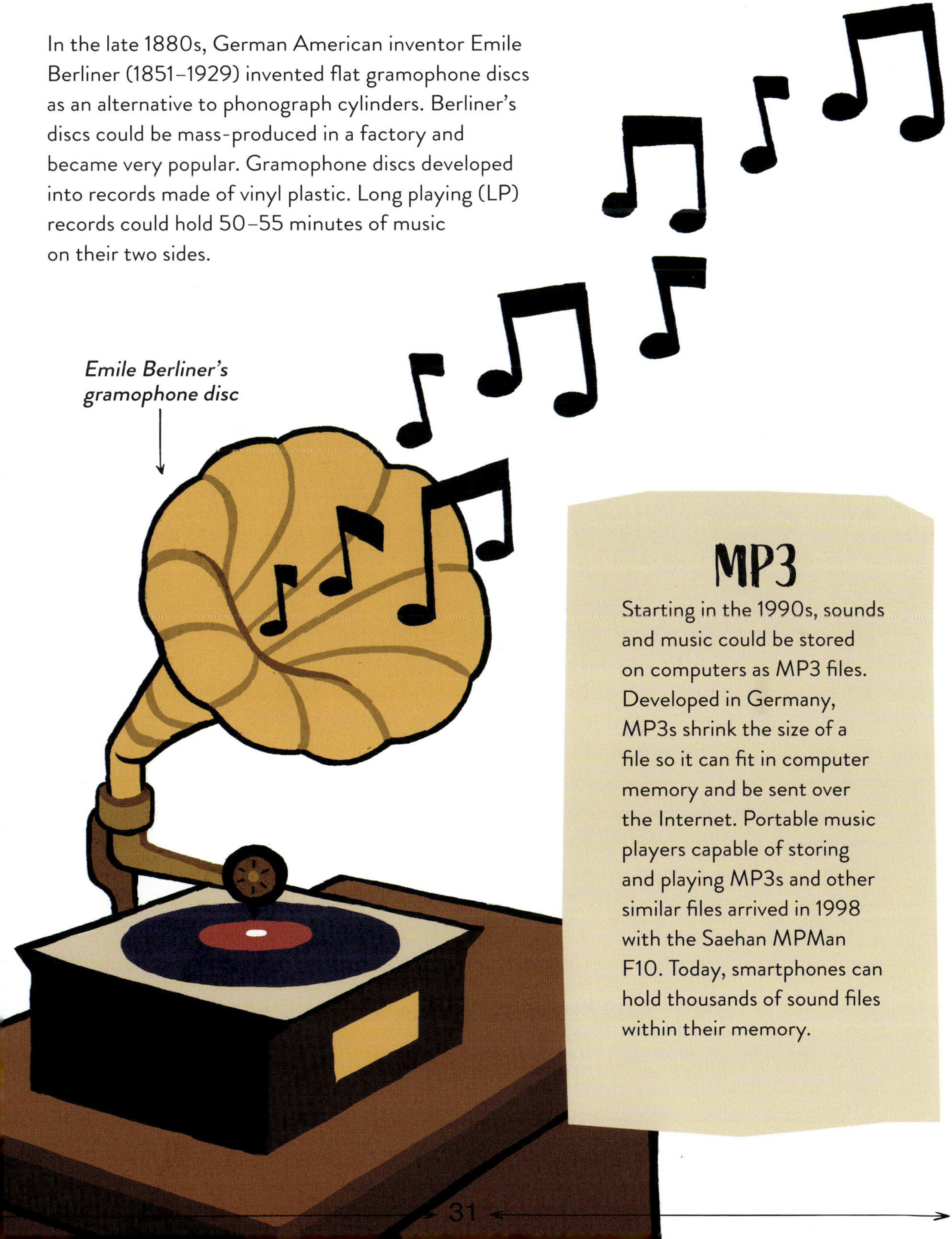

MP3

Starting in the 1990s, sounds and music could be stored on computers as MP3 files. Developed in Germany, MP3s shrink the size of a file so it can fit in computer memory and be sent over the Internet. Portable music players capable of storing and playing MP3s and other similar files arrived in 1998 with the Saehan MPMan F10. Today, smartphones can hold thousands of sound files within their memory.

Cinema

In the 19th century, doctors and scientists studied how the images our eyes see remain for a brief fraction of a second after they've been viewed. When a series of similar individual photos or images are shown quickly, one after another, they give the illusion of a moving scene.

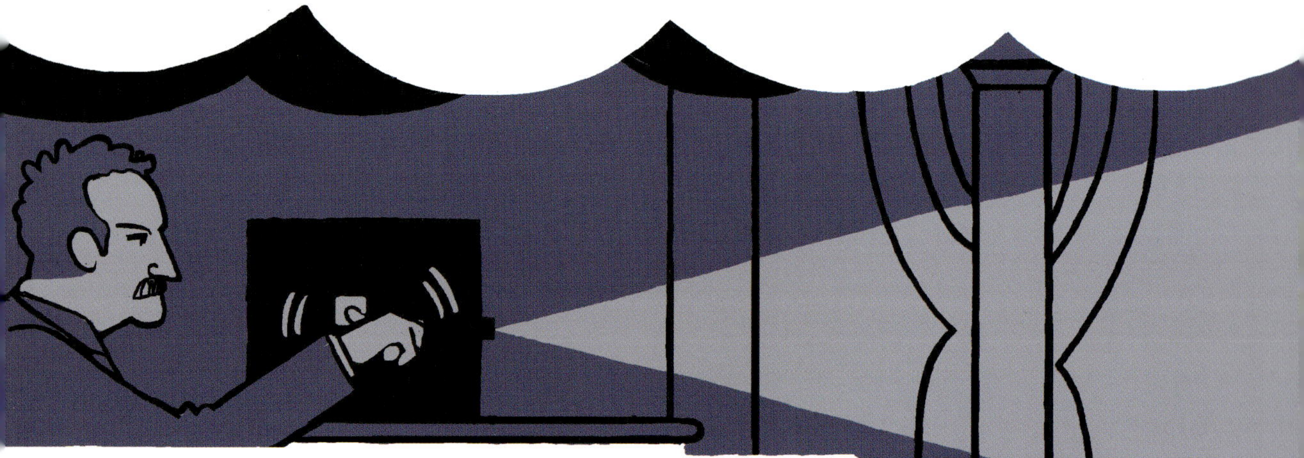

Thomas Edison was one of the first to turn this phenomenon into entertainment. He and William Dickson (1860–1935) invented the Kinetoscope between 1888 and 1892. Inside, long loops of film contained lots of individual photos. When an electric motor turned the loops, one person could look through an eyehole and view "moving" pictures (movies).

Computer Cartoons

Animated films were drawn by hand by dozens of artists until computers took on some of the workload. The first full-length film completely animated on computer was Pixar's *Toy Story* in 1995.

Inspired by the Kinetoscope, French brothers Louis (1864–1948) and Auguste Lumière (1862–1954) invented a device that allowed films to be enjoyed by several people at the same time. The Cinématographe worked first as a film camera, taking 16 photos every second. It could then play back the film as a projector, magnifying the scene on to a screen or wall.

The brothers debuted their short films, each lasting under a minute, in Paris in 1895. The next year, they opened Cinématographe theaters in London, Brussels, and New York. Filmmaking boomed with improved cameras and longer films. Early cinema goers might be entertained by a piano player that played music in time with the silent film. Sound and the actors speaking arrived in the 1920s.

Heavier-than-Air Aircraft

On December 17, 1903, in Kill Devil Hills, North Carolina, the first heavier-than-air powered aircraft took off. At the controls and lying on his stomach between the plane's two sets of wings was Orville Wright (1871–1948). His brother, Wilbur (1867–1912), crashed on his attempt three days earlier.

Wilbur Wright

The first flight of the Wright *Flyer* lasted 12 seconds and covered a distance of 120 feet (36.5 m). Three more flights were attempted that day. The longest, flown by Wilbur, lasted 59 seconds and covered 852 feet (259 m). It was a triumph for the brothers, who owned a bicycle shop but had long been fascinated by flight. The pair had made 200 flights in their own unpowered gliders to learn more about how air flowing under and over wings lifts planes into the air.

The brothers demonstrated new versions of their aircraft in Europe in 1908, sparking an aviation craze. Within a year, Frenchman Louis Blériot (1872–1936) flew a single-winged aircraft across the English Channel and aircraft developed quickly into many different types — from small, single-seat military fighter planes to passenger-carrying airliners with four or more engines.

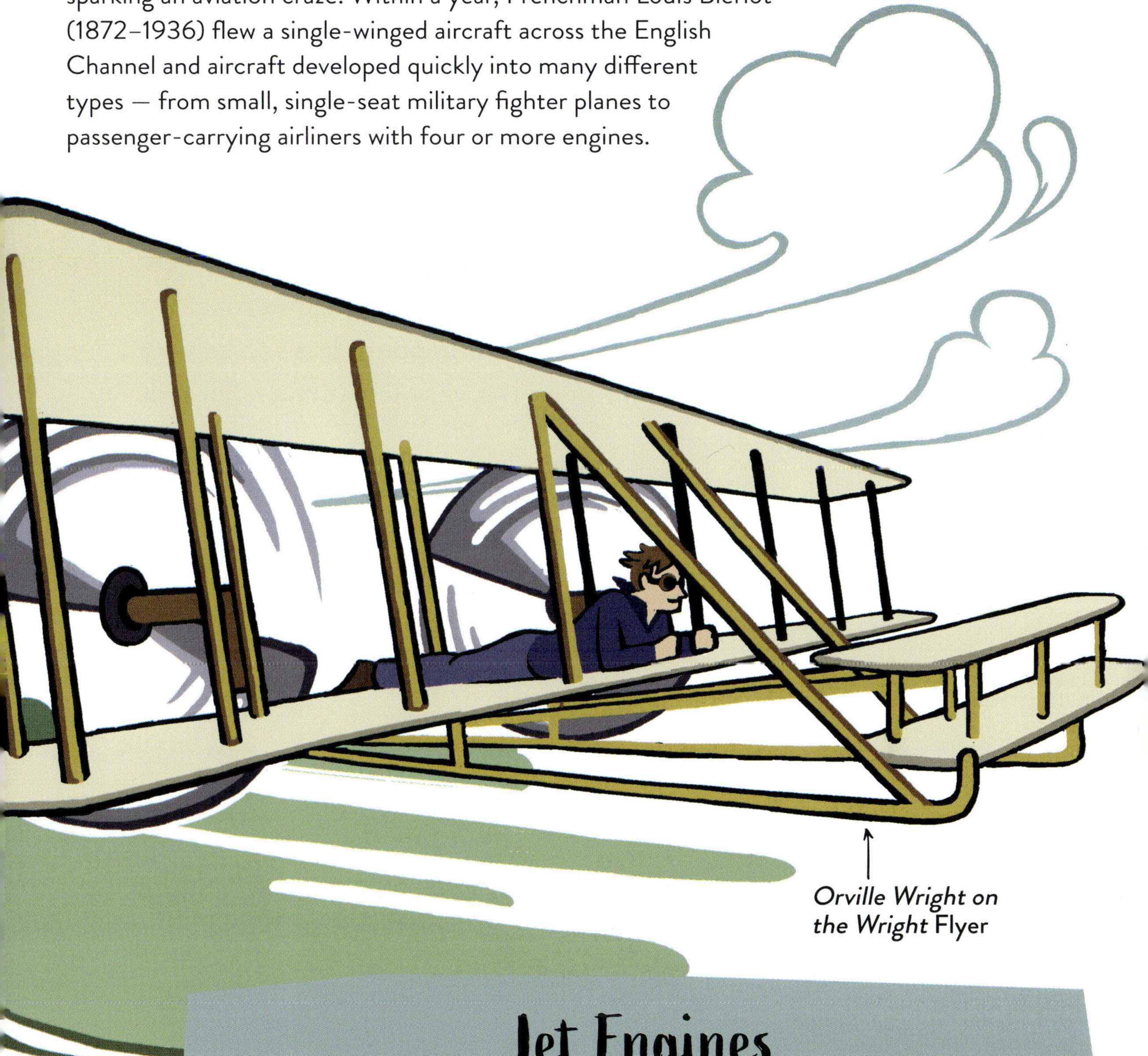

Orville Wright on the Wright Flyer

Jet Engines

Early aircraft were powered by car or motorbike engines that spun propellers to push the plane forward. The invention of jet engines in the 1930s provided planes with more power to fly higher and faster. Today the Airbus A380 airliner can carry up to 853 people on one flight lasting thousands of miles.

New Materials

As materials science developed in the 20th century, many exciting and useful substances were produced. One was invented by accident. Roy Plunkett (1910–94) was working at U.S. chemical company DuPont in 1938, trying to make new cooling gases for refrigerators. He discovered one of his gases, when cooled, left behind a white powder. The powder didn't react with other chemicals and had a high melting point. It was also very slippery — scientists would say it has very low surface friction.

Named PTFE* and better known as Teflon®, it proved handy for all sorts of tasks. Its slippery nature helped reduce friction in moving parts of machines. It also made a great covering for electrical wiring and repelled water so it was used in some waterproof clothing. French aircraft engineer Marc Grégoire used PTFE to coat pots and pans, inventing the first nonstick cookware in 1954.

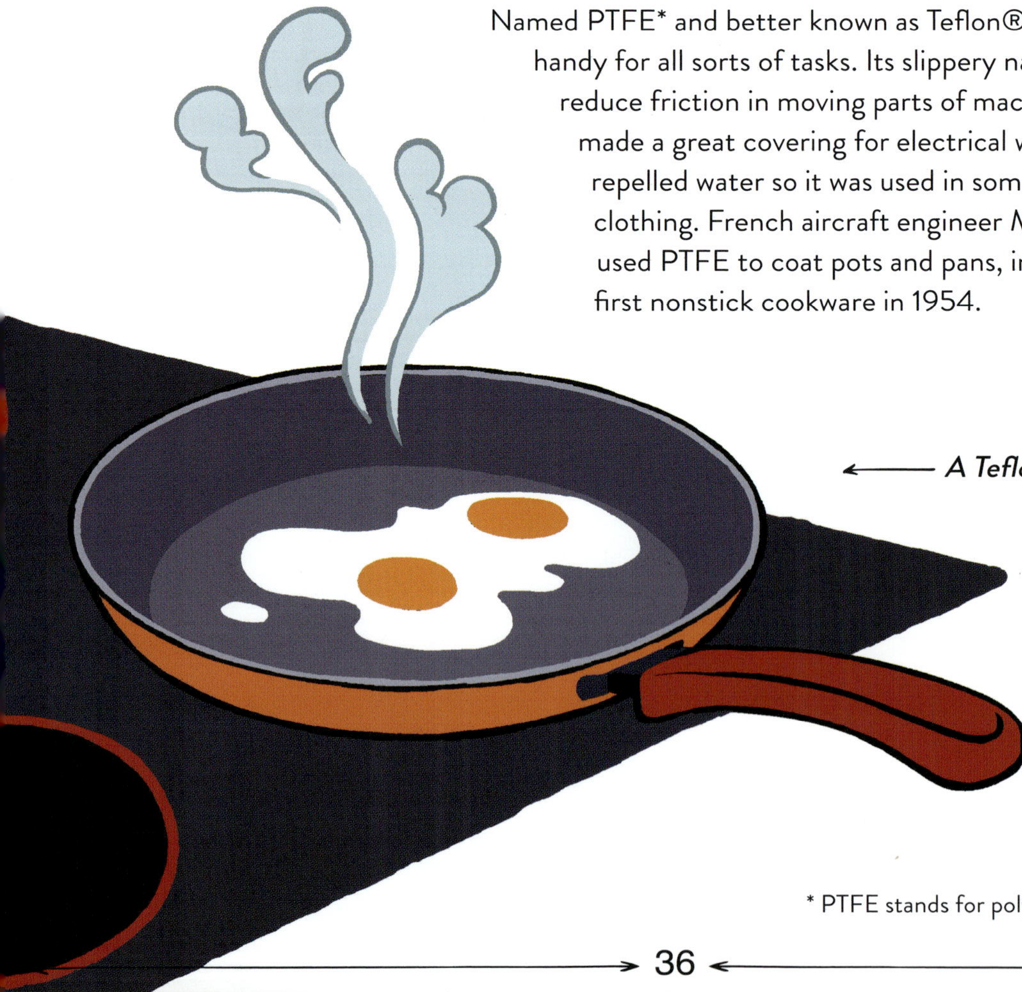

← *A Teflon® frying pan*

* PTFE stands for polytetrafluoroethylene

Stephanie Kwolek

Ten years later, another DuPont chemist, Stephanie Kwolek (1923–2014), was researching ways of making new ultra-strong and tough but lightweight fibers to strengthen car tires. She developed a very stiff, heat-resistant plastic fiber called Kevlar®. Fellow scientists were amazed at this wonder material. Unlike most plastics, it could withstand heat up to 842°F (450°C). It was also lightweight, yet at least five times stronger than steel.

Kevlar® is used as a strengthening material in many different objects, from tires and tennis racquets to aircraft wings and crash helmets. It has the strength to stop a bullet in its tracks, making it a vital part of bulletproof vests and body armor worn by police officers.

Professional motorcycle riders wear helmets that are strengthened with layers of Kevlar®.

Global Positioning System

In 1957, the first artificial satellite, called Sputnik 1, headed into space, where it orbited Earth for three months. Since that time, hundreds of satellites have been launched to investigate Earth from above or to relay TV or telephone signals between different parts of the planet. In the 1970s both the U.S, and the former Soviet Union developed systems of satellites to help people find their way.

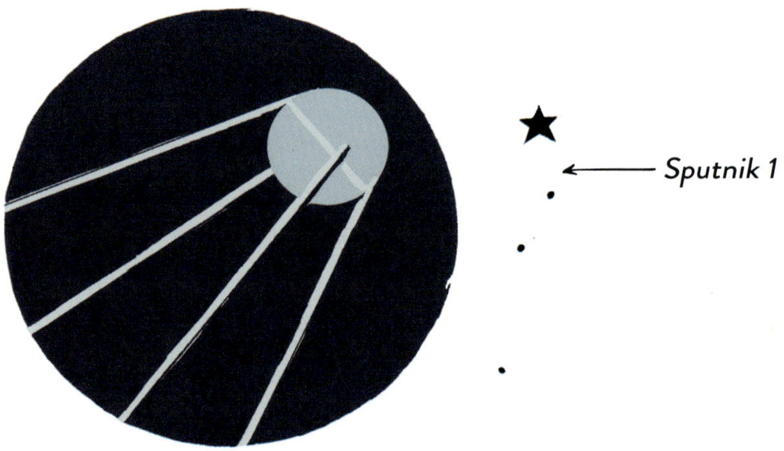

By 1993, more than 20 American NAVSTAR satellites formed the Global Positioning System (GPS). These orbit 12,550 miles (20,200 km) above Earth and keep track of their own precise position. Back on Earth, a device called a GPS receiver picks up radio signals from a group of these satellites at the same time. The receiver measures the time it takes for each of the satellite signals to reach it. From this information it can work out its own precise location on Earth to within a few yards.

GPS receivers were first carried by military forces and adventurers and were later installed in cars, trucks, and boats as satellite navigation systems. As technology advanced, GPS receivers shrank in size, so they could be fitted inside watches and smartphones. Some fitness watches use GPS to track how far a person has walked, run, or cycled during an exercise session.

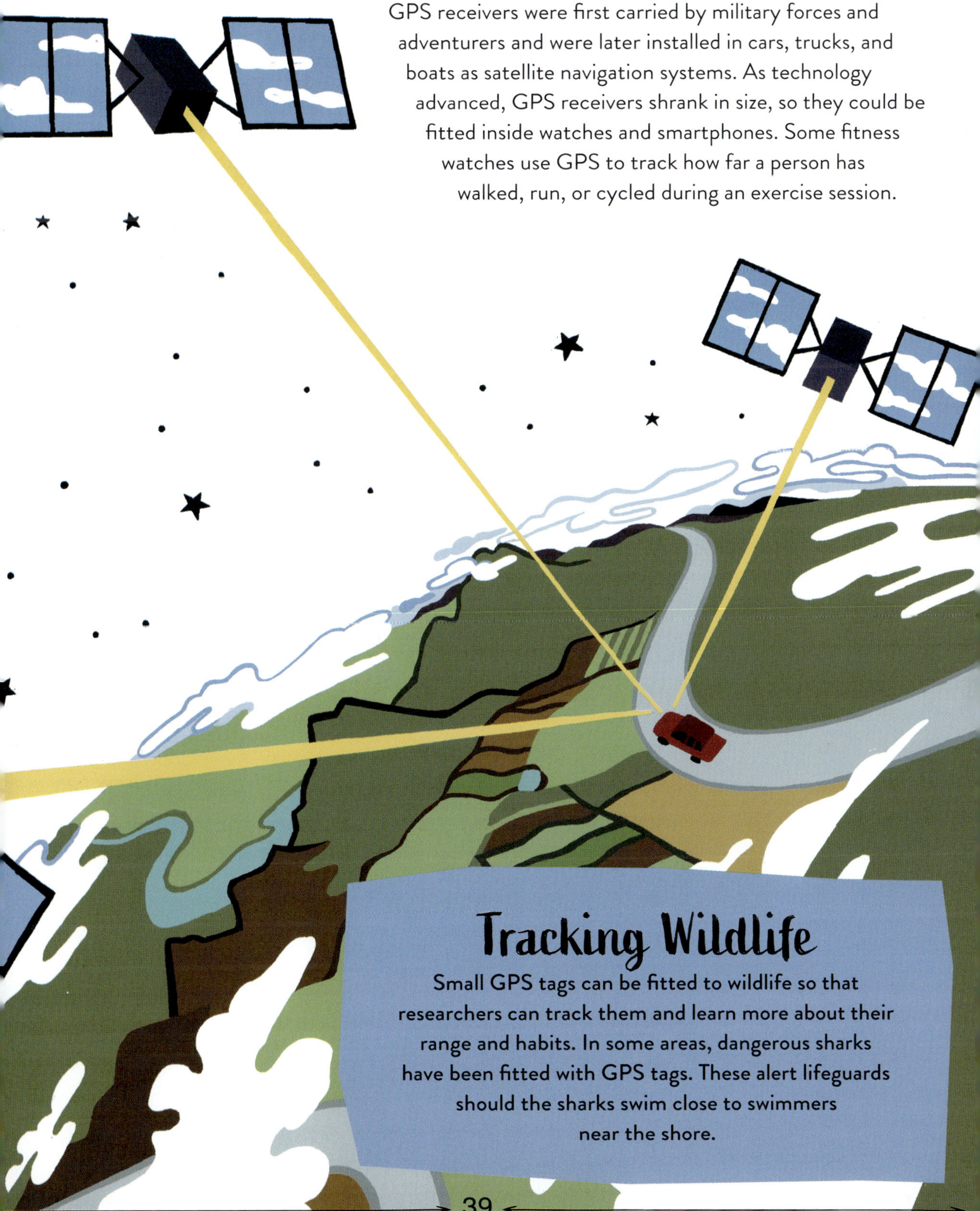

Tracking Wildlife

Small GPS tags can be fitted to wildlife so that researchers can track them and learn more about their range and habits. In some areas, dangerous sharks have been fitted with GPS tags. These alert lifeguards should the sharks swim close to swimmers near the shore.

Lasers

Lasers are powerful beams of concentrated light. In the 1940s and 1950s, scientists knew that lasers could exist in theory, but they struggled to build a practical working model.

In 1960, American engineer Theodore H. Maiman (1927–2007) had a breakthrough. He used a rod made of ruby crystal placed inside a type of flash lamp used in photography. When the flash produced a brilliant burst of light, the atoms in the ruby rod were agitated and gave out energy that escaped from the rod as a beam of red light — the first working laser.

Regular light, such as sunlight or the beam of a flashlight, contains a mix of all colors and spreads out the farther it travels. Lasers consist of just one color of light, which travels in straight lines without spreading out and weakening. This makes lasers great at measuring long distances accurately. In 1969, Apollo 11 astronauts put a reflector on the moon that bounced back a laser aimed at it from Earth. This gave scientists a very accurate distance between Earth and the moon.

A laser light show ⟶

Different colors and strengths of lasers were developed after Maiman's invention. Some are used to scan barcodes. Others are found inside media players to read the information on a CD or DVD. Powerful lasers are used in industry to cut through metal accurately or in medicine to act as a precise surgical tool to seal blood vessels or to correct eye problems. The first laser eye surgery on a human patient was performed in 1988 by American doctor Stephen Trokel (1934–).

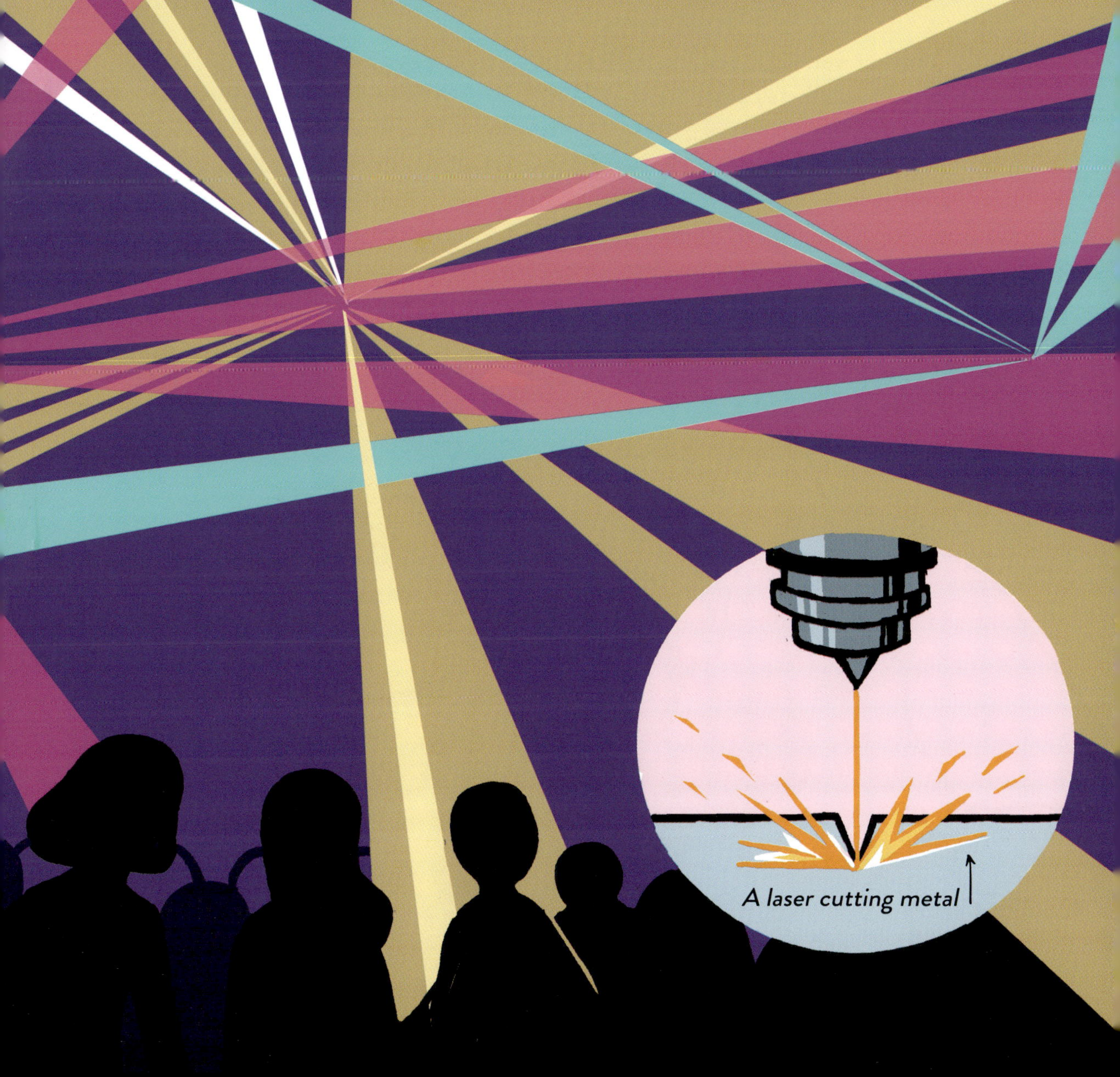

A laser cutting metal

Robots

Robots are incredible machines that can be given jobs to do, which they perform with little or no human help. Some can repeat the same task over and over again with perfect precision. This makes them ideal for jobs in factories, such as spray-painting, welding, and assembling products.

The first working robot was the Unimate invented by George Devol (1912–2011) and Joseph Engelberger (1925–2015). It was put to work in 1961 picking up and handling hot metal parts up to 330 pounds (150 kg) in weight in a U.S. car factory. The two-ton robot performed 100,000 hours of work before it was retired in 1971.

Unimate was a multi-jointed robot arm that could be programmed to perform tasks that were unpleasant or difficult for humans. It could also work for long periods without breaks. Unimate and similar robots built by others became popular with carmakers and then other manufacturing industries all over the world.

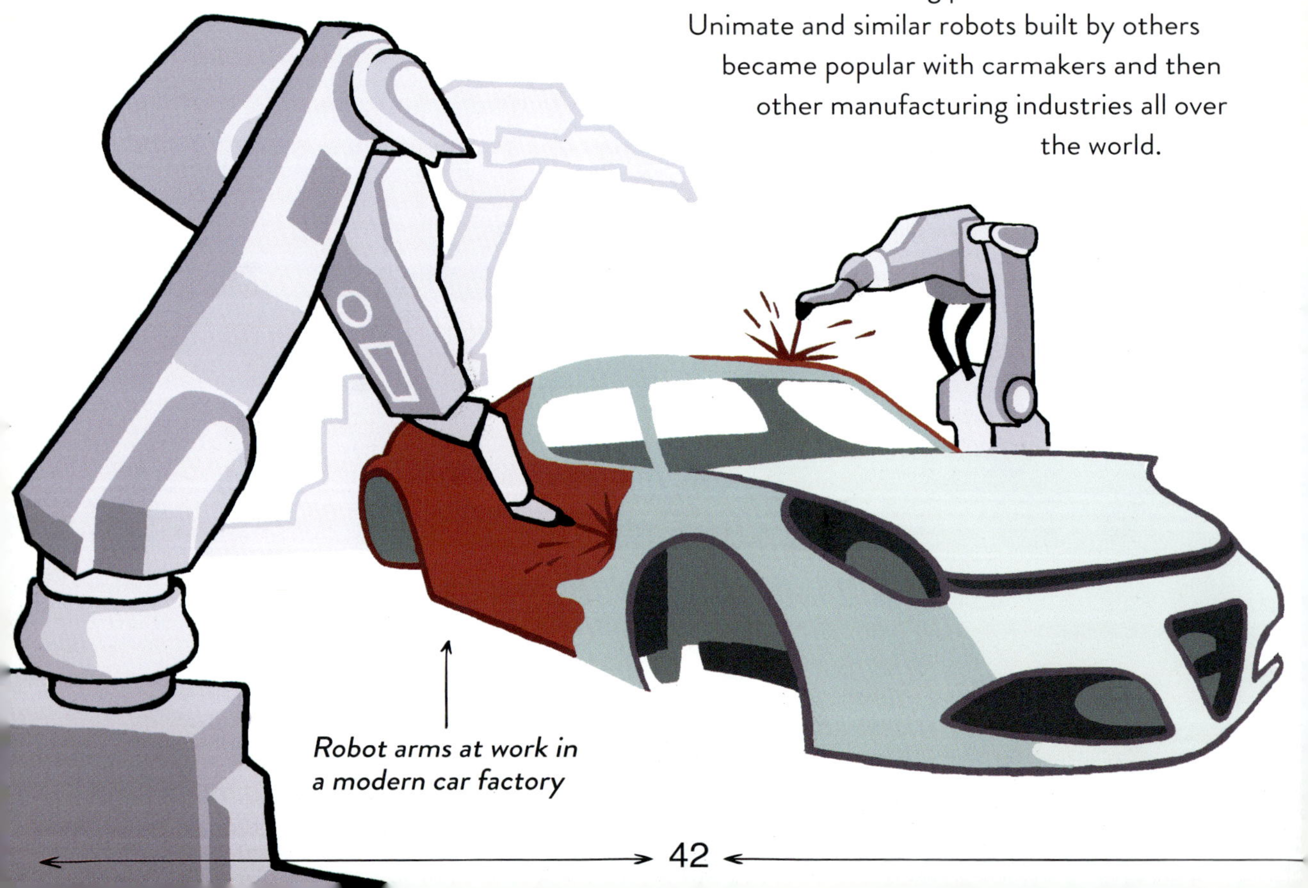

Robot arms at work in a modern car factory

The first robot able to move and find its own way was Shakey, developed by Stanford Research Institute, in California, in 1966. It used a TV camera to recognize a room and bounced beams of light off obstacles in its path to measure their distance away. Vacuum-cleaning robots using similar sensors debuted 30 years later. Robot vacuum cleaners, able to clean an entire floor of a house on their own, have become the world's most common robot with over 20 million sold.

Bomb Disposal

The first bomb disposal robot, called the Wheelbarrow, was invented by retired British army officer Peter Miller (1912–2006) in 1972. Bomb disposal robots save lives because they can examine and, sometimes, defuse bombs and handle dangerous objects.

Some robots have been sent to places that are impossible or too dangerous for humans to visit. In 1997, NASA's Sojourner became the first moving robot to explore another planet, Mars. Three years earlier, the eight-legged Dante II robot climbed into the mouth of Mount Spurr, an active volcano in Alaska.

World Wide Web

In the 1980s, British computer programmer Tim Berners-Lee (1955–) worked at a huge science research center called CERN in Switzerland. It contained 10,000 scientists and hundreds of different projects — and keeping track of everyone and everything proved very confusing.

Berners-Lee had experimented with hyperlinks in the past to make a computerized address book at CERN called ENQUIRE. Clicking on a hyperlink on the screen called up a new screen full of information. He thought that a similar system could be used worldwide, so that people using any computer could access and share not just contact details, but any information from anywhere in the world over the Internet.

By the end of 1990, Berners-Lee and his colleagues had built all the parts of their new information system. They thought about calling it The Mesh or The Information Mine (TIM), but instead chose World Wide Web (WWW). Webpages of text and images were made by coding documents using a language called HTML (hypertext markup language). A collection of webpages (a website) were then stored on a web server computer. This could send any of the webpages to another computer when a user clicked on a hyperlink or typed the webpage name into a web browser — a program also invented by Berners-Lee.

Tim Berners-Lee →

Anyone with a computer, web browser, and Internet access could view the first website from the summer of 1991. The Web grew slowly at first (there were only 130 websites two years later), but then it exploded. Today, more than a billion websites exist.

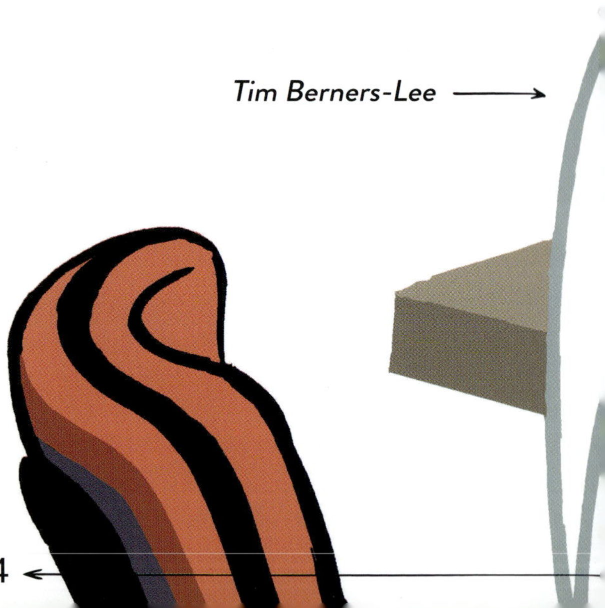

Digital technology is certainly at the forefront of many new inventions, but innovations are being made in all areas of expertise. One of the most exciting things about the future is that we don't yet know what these new inventions will look like, or even what they might do! With enough imagination, creativity, and technical know-how, you might be the next world-famous inventor.

Glossary

app Short for application, small computer programs that let you complete a task, such as a game or a sound file player

artificial Made or produced by people and not found in nature

biodegrade Decomposing naturally, usually as a result of bacteria or other organisms

furrow A long, narrow trench in the ground

hide The skin of an animal

Internet A global network of computer networks through which computers communicate by sending information

laser Short for light amplification by stimulated emission of radiation, this is a form of single-color concentrated light that travels in straight lines

loom A machine that makes fabric by weaving thread

medieval The Middle Ages; CE 1100–1453

microchip A tiny piece of silicon on which are etched large numbers of electronic circuits

microprocessor A large collection of microscopic electrical circuits all fitted on to a single wafer of silicon to create an entire computing system on a chip

network A connection between two or more computers that enables them to communicate

nomadic Describes people who do not have a permanent home but continually travel from place to place

orbit The act of traveling around a body in space, such as a planet, a moon, or a star like the sun

patent The right for an inventor to stop others from making their invention without their agreement

prototype An experimental design of part or all of a machine built for testing

PTFE Short for polytetrafluoroethylene, this slippery substance is used to reduce friction in machines and as a coating on nonstick pans

satellite An object that orbits a planet or another body. Artificial satellites often orbit Earth and perform useful tasks, such as broadcasting TV pictures around the world

sensor A device that gives a robot information about itself or its surroundings